DATE DUE

Children
of a
NEW CENTURY

Children
of a
NEW CENTURY

Jane A. Schott

Carolrhoda Books, Inc./Minneapolis

In loving memory of my father, Karl Harvey Schott (1908–1969), a child in the new century

Page one: Feeding the chickens was a common chore for children in the early 1900s.
Page two: A boy photographs a successful fishing trip in Kansas in 1902.
Opposite page: Dr. J. N. McCormack (at right in bow tie) demonstrates a new product to visitors to the Kentucky State Fair in 1913.

Text copyright © 1999 by Carolrhoda Books, Inc.

All rights reserved. International copyright secured. No part of this book may be reproduced, stored in a retrieval system, or transmitted in any form or by any means, electronic, mechanical, photocopying, recording, or otherwise, without the prior written permission of Carolrhoda Books, Inc., except for the inclusion of brief quotations in an acknowledged review.

Carolrhoda Books, Inc., c/o The Lerner Publishing Group
241 First Avenue North, Minneapolis, MN 55401 U.S.A.

Website address: www.lernerbooks.com

LIBRARY OF CONGRESS CATALOGING-IN-PUBLICATION

Schott, Jane A., 1946-
   Children of a new century / Jane A. Schott.
     p.   cm. — (Picture the American past)
   Includes bibliographical references (p.   ) and index.
   Summary: Describes how children dressed, played, learned, and worked in the early 1900s and how new inventions were changing their lives.
   ISBN 1-57505-220-2
   1. Children—United States—Social conditions—Juvenile literature. 2. Children—United States—History—20th century—Juvenile literature. 3. United States—Social conditions—1865–1918—Juvenile literature. 4. United States—Social life and customs—1865–1918—Juvenile literature. 5. United States—History—1901–1909—Juvenile literature. [1. United States—Social life and customs—1865–1918.]
I. Title. II. Series.
HQ792.U5S364 1999
305.23'0973—dc21   98-14099

Manufactured in the United States of America
1 2 3 4 5 6 – JR – 04 03 02 01 00 99

CONTENTS

Above: A crowd of people, young and old, gathers to watch a car race down a road in the early 1900s.

Opposite page: A child sits on the running board of a truck in Cleveland, Ohio.

A New Century

Meet me in St. Louis, Louis,
Meet me at the fair.
Don't tell me the lights are shining
Any place but there!
—words to "Meet Me in St. Louis, Louis,"
a popular song written in 1904

On the last day of 1899, grown-ups and children everywhere were excited. They were celebrating the start of a new century. The 1800s were ending, and the 1900s were beginning.

Life was quickly changing. Boys and girls talked and wondered about new automobiles that could go faster than a horse and telephones that could carry a voice over a wire!

St. Louis, Missouri. Visitors crowd around displays of new inventions, such as these electric lamps.

In 1904, a great fair opened in St. Louis, Missouri. At night, the fair was brightly lit with more than half a million electric bulbs. In the Palace of Electricity, you could see inventions that ran on electricity. You could make a call to Chicago or Kansas City on telephones. In the Palace of Transportation, you could see 140 automobiles that had come from as far away as Boston.

Grown-ups and children saw inventions that would make life easier in the new century. They tried new foods like hot dogs, ice-cream cones, peanut butter, and cotton candy. If they were thirsty, they might have tried a new drink invented at the fair— ice tea.

St. Louis, Missouri. Children at the World's Fair sample a newfangled treat—ice-cream cones!

Although children and parents enjoyed seeing electric lights and automobiles at the fair, most Americans did not yet have these things. But almost everyone wished to have them!

Boonville, Missouri. In the early 1900s, most people still got around on horseback or in horse-drawn wagons, not in automobiles.

Lewiston, Montana. A boy proudly poses for a photograph, taking the wheel of the parked family car.

The first automobiles were expensive. They were also difficult to drive and needed to be repaired often. Only rich people could afford them.

Cincinnati, Ohio. Children board a streetcar on their way to a picnic.

In most cities, people used streetcars to travel around. A street-car ran on rails and had seats for many people. The first streetcars were pulled by horses. Later, cities began to use electric streetcars. You could ride the streetcar downtown for about five cents.

Lindstrom, Minnesota. For fun, children wave at a passing express train.

The fastest way to travel a long distance was by train. By 1900, two hundred thousand miles of railroad tracks crisscrossed America. Trains carried people, animals, and all kinds of supplies. A farmer could order baby chicks to be sent by train. Children from Ohio might visit their grandmother in New York by train.

Two boys, warmly dressed for winter, bring home a Christmas tree in the early 1900s.

Whether they traveled or stayed home, children in the early 1900s dressed differently than modern children. Boys wore short pants, called knickers, and knee-high socks. Girls wore long socks, too, and dresses. Almost everyone wore a hat.

Girls braided or pinned up their long hair. Boys wore their hair short. Mom or Dad was usually the "barber," and haircuts were often not quite even.

Near the end of summer, children got ready to go back to school. New shoes might be ordered from a catalog. Mothers sewed many of the clothes their children wore.

A well-dressed group of children listens as one girl reads a magazine.

Westerville, Ohio. These boys ride a pony to school. Then they tie the pony to the school's hitching post. The pony will wait patiently until the end of the school day.

School Days,
Work, and Play

School days, school days,
Dear old golden rule days,
Readin' and 'ritin' and 'rithmetic,
Taught to the tune of a hick'ry stick.
—words to "School Days,"
a popular song written in 1906

Early in the 1900s, most children did not ride a bus to school. In the country, some children walked several miles along dusty, muddy, or snowy roads. Others rode horses or ponies.

Children in towns or cities could walk on sidewalks or the edge of the street. But they had to watch where they stepped and keep from being splashed with muddy water by passing buggies and wagons and automobiles.

Only the bigger city schools had a classroom for each grade. Many schools had only one room.

Students learned to read, write, spell, and do arithmetic. They also had lessons in geography, history, good manners, and the Bible. The teacher was usually strict. Students who misbehaved were sometimes hit with a stick or leather strap.

Children in this city classroom study Indians, or Native Americans.

Children at a country school play at recess.

At recess, London Bridge, Farmer in the Dell, and Fox and Geese were popular games. Boys liked baseball, sometimes played with a stick and a homemade ball. Girls practiced jumping rope and played hopscotch.

Shooting marbles was a favorite way to spend a Saturday.

Most children did not have many toys, but they enjoyed playing games. Boys especially liked playing marbles. Players collected shiny glass marbles in solid and mixed colors. When the game was for "keeps," players sometimes lost their favorite marbles. Then they would try to win the marbles back in the next game.

Only a few schools or parks had real swings, a teeter-totter, or a slide. So children made their own fun. A board and a box could make a teeter-totter. A rope, a board, and a strong tree limb could make a swing.

Leavenworth, Kansas. These girls make the most of a teeter-totter.

Coney Island, New York. Boys race on Coney Island's steeplechase ride.

A few big cities had amusement parks. At Coney Island in New York, you could walk for a mile on the boardwalk. You could throw a ball to win a prize, ride the roller coaster or merry-go-round, or swim in the ocean.

If you had five cents, you could go to the movies on Saturday. The pictures were in black and white, and there was no sound. A piano or organ played throughout the movie. During exciting parts, the music was fast and loud. During quiet parts, it was slow and soft.

New York City. In the early 1900s, going to the movies was a special treat.

A boy struggles to do his chores.

Children enjoyed movies and games. But they also had chores to do at home.

Children helped their mothers sweep the floors, beat the rugs, wash clothes in a tub, and hang them outside on a line to dry. They helped cut firewood and carry it to the stove or fireplace. They also pumped water and carried it to the kitchen.

Children who lived on farms worked especially hard. In winter, they got up early to feed the chickens, cows, and horses before school. In summer, they spent long hours working in the fields. One woman remembers, "Making hay was the hottest, hardest work I had to do when I was a child."

Girls take a needed rest from making hay.

Westerville, Ohio. Working a field with a one-horse team could take a long time. In this photograph, Karl Harvey Schott, the author's father, takes a break.

In spring, fields had to be plowed. When the soil was ready for planting, farm families worked from sunup until sundown. In fall, everyone felt proud when the crops were harvested. They would help feed a growing country.

San Francisco, California. Children came to America from many parts of the world. These two young immigrants in California came from China.

In the early 1900s, many new people came to America from around the world. These immigrants wanted better homes and better jobs.

The newcomers usually lived together and did not speak English. But their children went to school. They made friends and learned the new language. Often children taught parents their first words of English.

McDonald, West Virginia. This boy works in a coal mine all day.

   Most parents wanted their children to go to school. But some families were so poor, the children had to work to help pay the bills.
   Some boys worked in coal mines. The mines were damp and dusty and dangerous. A cave-in could bury workers deep below the ground. When the mine whistle blew an emergency blast, mothers and sisters and others came running. Sometimes miners were never rescued.

Many children worked in cotton mills all day long. Girls as young as six or seven walked up and down the long rows of spinners, watching for breaks in threads. When the girls found a break, they quickly tied the threads together.

Many working children never learned to read and write. But in the new century, the United States would pass laws to keep children in school and out of dangerous jobs.

North Pownal, Vermont. This girl checks cotton spinners in a mill.

Long Island, New York. Theodore Roosevelt, shown with his family at their summer house, became president of the United States in 1901.

Country and Family

My father's name is Theodore Roosevelt and—
well, he is "it."
—twelve-year-old Kermit Roosevelt,
describing his father to his classmates

In 1901, Theodore Roosevelt became the 26th president of the United States. Most Americans thought he did a good job, and in 1904, Roosevelt was elected to another term.

Roosevelt had six children. While he was president, the White House was full of children and their pets. The president thought it was important for children to care for something. Dogs, tadpoles, turtles, kangaroo rats, flying squirrels, a badger, and a pony lived at the White House.

President Roosevelt loved nature and often took his children hiking and camping. He wanted to make sure that all Americans could enjoy forests, lakes and rivers, and wildlife. While he was president, over one million acres of forests were added to national forest lands.

Olympic Peninsula, Washington. Camping was one way for Americans to have fun outdoors. Here Glen Bigdrew and Ed Moon eat by their tent.

A group picnics by the family car in about 1915.

Americans loved seeing America. Families wanted cars so they could take trips.

When Henry Ford sold the first Model T Ford in 1908, it cost $850. That was more money than most people earned in a whole year. But Ford figured out how to make cars more quickly and cheaply. Soon families could buy a Model T for only $290.

Early in the new century, most Americans believed that if you worked hard you could have what you wanted—including a Model T Ford. But for some Americans, it was not that easy.

African Americans had a difficult time getting good jobs, homes, and an education. Laws did not always protect the rights of black people. Black children weren't allowed to attend most schools with white children. Schools for black children were often crowded and had few books.

Florida. Black students and teachers pose for a photograph. Their school is overcrowded, and the roof leaks in many places.

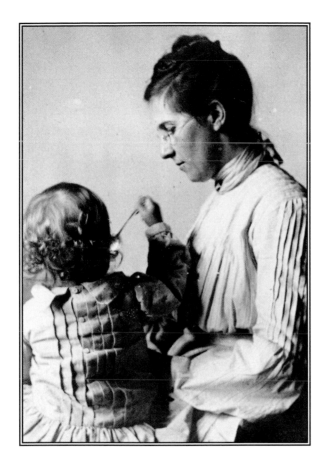

Wisconsin. In the early 1900s, a child takes a dose of medicine.

In the early 1900s, many medicines had not yet been discovered. Sometimes children died from diseases that can now be easily cured.

Doctors were finding ways to help children stay healthy. New medicines were important. But children were also taught that germs can cause illness. Children learned to wash their hands before eating and to cover their mouth when coughing.

Kansas City, Missouri. First graders take part in a toothbrush drill.

Children were taught how to take care of their teeth, too. Some schools even held toothbrush drills!

Westerville, Ohio. A mother and her daughters dress up in their best clothes to have their picture taken together.

Mothers cared for children when they were well and when they were sick. Most mothers did not work at a job away from home. They were expected to stay home and take care of their families. In 1914, a special day was set aside to honor mothers. We still celebrate Mother's Day on the second Sunday in May.

In the early 1900s, most Americans thought the United States was a peaceful place to live. But in Europe, people were fighting and being killed. World War I was beginning. In 1917, the United States joined the fighting. Brothers, uncles, and fathers would soon go off to war. Children helped out however they could.

Cooperstown, New York. These boys knit scarves and socks for soldiers in World War I.

For American children in the early 1900s, the Fourth of July was a favorite holiday—and a great day for waving a flag.

At the beginning of the new century, America had been a country for only 124 years. Life would change quickly over the next 100 years, but some things stayed the same. Already, the Fourth of July was a favorite holiday for many children. When the children of the new century saw flags flying and fireworks flashing across the night sky, they felt proud to be Americans.

A Turn-of-the-Century Game

How to Play Marbles

Children at the turn of the last century loved playing games as much as modern children do. Marbles was one of the most popular games of the early 1900s. Playing marbles is easy and fun. There are lots of different ways to play, but here are rules for a game called Ringer, or Ringers. Ringer is also sometimes called Ring Taw. (*Taw* is another word for shooter marble.)

Each year in June, participants in the National Marbles Tournament play Ringer. They play according to somewhat different rules than those described here. Players must be 14 years old or younger to participate. For more information, write to National Marbles Tournament, 810 Rayne Drive, Cumberland, MD 21502.

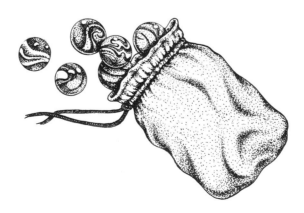

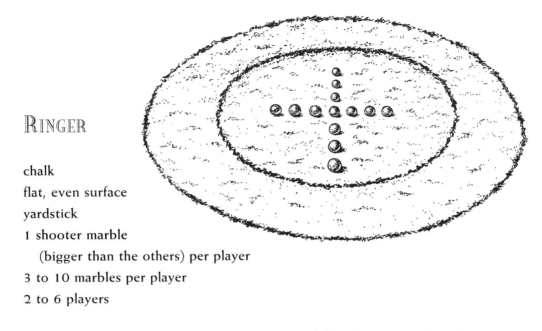

Ringer

chalk
flat, even surface
yardstick
1 shooter marble
   (bigger than the others) per player
3 to 10 marbles per player
2 to 6 players

1. Using chalk, draw a circle on playground blacktop or other flat, even surface. Measure to make sure the circle is two feet across.

2. Draw another circle around the first one, centering the first circle inside the second one. Measure to make sure the second circle is six feet across. The larger circle will mark your shooting line.

3. Each player places an equal number of marbles in the smaller circle. Arrange the marbles to form an X shape in the center.

4. The first player places a shooter marble at the edge of the larger circle. Then that player shoots the marble toward the others in the smaller circle. Any marbles that the shooter knocks out of the smaller circle are captured by the player.

5. If the shooter rolls out of the smaller circle, the player's turn is over. If the shooter stops inside the smaller circle but has not knocked out any of the marbles, then the player's turn is also over. (Leave the shooter where it is; the player will shoot from that spot on his or her next turn.)

6. The player can shoot again if the shooter stops inside the smaller circle and knocks marbles out. The player captures any marbles knocked out of the smaller circle.

7. The first player continues until the shooter goes outside the smaller circle or until the shooter fails to knock marbles out of the smaller circle. Then the next player takes a turn.

8. The winner is the player who has the most marbles after all the marbles are knocked out of the smaller circle.

Note: If your shooter is still inside the smaller circle at the end of your turn and is later knocked out of the smaller circle by another player, that player cannot capture your shooter. You will shoot from your shooter's position on your next turn.

Note to Teachers and Adults

For children, the early 1900s may seem like part of a far-off past. But there are many ways to make this era and its people come alive. Along with helping children learn to play marbles, you can help them explore America's turn-of-the-century past in other ways. One way is for them to read more about the era. More books on the topic are listed on pages 45 and 46. Another way you can help young readers explore the past is to train them to study historical photographs. Historical photographs hold many clues about how life was lived in earlier times. Ask your children or students to look for the details and "read" all the information in each picture in this book. For example, how do the clothes worn by boys and girls in the photos on pages 2, 9, 15, and 21 differ from clothes worn by modern boys and girls?

To encourage young readers to learn to read historical photographs, have them try these activities:

Getting Around

Look at the photographs of people going from place to place in the early 1900s. On a piece of paper in one column, under the heading "early 1900s," list the ways people got around at the turn of the last century. Next, set aside time in the evening or on a weekend to interview your parents or other adults. Ask them how they traveled from place to place when they were young. List your findings in a second column, under the heading "my parents' day." In a third column, under the heading "my day," list the ways you travel. Have some ways of getting around stayed the same over time? Have others changed? How do you think children will travel in the future?

Having Fun

The photographs on pages 19 through 23 of this book show children having fun. Study the photographs and make a list of all the things children are doing. Then make a list of your favorite things to do for fun. Ask yourself what inventions make these activities possible. How many of the activities on your list depend on inventions? How many activities in the early 1900s depended on inventions? What conclusions can you draw? Have inventions changed the ways in which we have fun? In a few sentences, sum up your findings.

Growing Up with the Century

Dress in costume and tell your friends, parents, or classmates what it was like to grow up in the early 1900s. Read the text—and the photos—in this book for information and details about daily life. To add to your presentation, read some of the books about the turn of the last century listed on pages 45 and 46. If you are playing the part of a child in the city, take a look at Barbara Cooney's *Hattie and the Wild Waves* or Lisa Griest's *Lost at the White House*. If you are playing the part of a child living in a small town, read Mary Downing Hahn's *Time for Andrew*, Ouida Sebestyen's *Words by Heart*, or Michael Tunnell's *Mailing May*.

Your Town's Past

Contact your local historical society to find photographs, maps, or prints of your town or city in the early 1900s. Did your town even exist at the turn of the last century? If so, does your town look the same as it does in old photographs? If you have a camera, take pictures of the same places shown in old photographs of your town. Then create a display comparing views of the past and the present.

Resources on the Turn of the Century

Cooney, Barbara. *Hattie and the Wild Waves: A Story from Brooklyn.* New York: Viking, 1990. In this picture book, author and illustrator Cooney re-creates her mother's privileged childhood in the early 1900s.

Griest, Lisa. *Lost at the White House: A 1909 Easter Story.* Minneapolis, Minn.: Carolrhoda Books, Inc., 1994. While attending the annual White House Easter egg roll, nine-year-old Rena becomes lost in President Taft's home.

Hahn, Mary Downing. *Time for Andrew: A Ghost Story.* New York: Clarion Books, 1994. On a visit to the family homestead in Missouri, Drew Tyler meets a ghost—a boy named Andrew, who lived in 1910.

Hakim, Joy. *An Age of Extremes.* New York: Oxford University Press, 1994. Part of a series of books on United States history, this volume covers the years from 1880 until the beginning of World War I.

Hyatt, Patricia Rusch. *Coast to Coast with Alice.* Minneapolis, Minn.: Carolrhoda Books, Inc., 1995. Author Hyatt mixes fact with fiction when she re-creates the diary entries of Minna Jahns, a real-life 16-year-old girl who took part in a coast-to-coast car trip in 1909.

Levinson, Nancy Smiler. *Turn of the Century: Our Nation One Hundred Years Ago.* New York: Lodestar Books, 1994. Levinson describes the people of America in the early 1900s, from the wealthy owners of railroads and factories, to the immigrants, to the farmers of the American West.

Schulz, Walter A. *Will and Orv.* Minneapolis, Minn.: Carolrhoda Books, Inc., 1991. In 1903, five people—four men and a boy named Johnny Moore—witnessed the Wright brothers' first flight. Author Schulz imagines what the first powered flight must have been like, seen through the eyes of Johnny Moore.

Sebestyen, Ouida. *Words by Heart.* Boston: Little, Brown and Company, An Atlantic Monthly Press Book, 1979. Lena Sills wins a scripture-quoting contest, but not everyone in Bethel Springs is happy to see a black girl win the top prize. Set in 1910, this novel tells a story of growing up and overcoming prejudice.

Snyder, Zilpha Keatley. *Gib Rides Home.* New York: Delacorte Press, 1998. In this novel, Gib Whittaker leaves the orphanage to take care of horses at the Rocking M Ranch. The few months Gib spends there, from 1908 to 1909, prove to be a time of confusion, changes, and challenges.

Tunnell, Michael O. Illustrated by Ted Rand. *Mailing May.* New York: Greenwillow Books, A Tambourine Book, 1997. This picture book, set in Idaho in 1914, is based on the true story of a young girl named May, who takes an unusual trip to see her grandmother.

Yep, Lawrence. *Dragonwings.* New York: Harper & Row, Publishers, 1975. In this novel set in 1903, a Chinese boy joins his father in San Francisco's Chinatown. Together, they dream of building and flying an airplane.

Website   http://lcweb2.loc.gov/detroit/dethome.html
Take a tour of turn-of-the-century America by viewing photographs and postcards from the Detroit Publishing Company from the 1880s to 1920.

New Words

century: a period of one hundred years. Officially, a century starts after the previous one-hundred-year period has ended, so the 1900s began on January 1, 1901. People at the time, however, celebrated the turn of the century at midnight on December 31, 1899.

immigrants: people who come to live in a new country

knickers: short pants that come to just below the knees

streetcar: a large, single car that runs on rails and carries many people

turn of the century: the beginning of a new period of one hundred years. See *century* above.

Index

TIME LINE

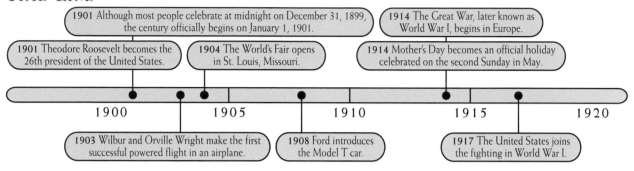

1901 Although most people celebrate at midnight on December 31, 1899, the century officially begins on January 1, 1901.

1914 The Great War, later known as World War I, begins in Europe.

1901 Theodore Roosevelt becomes the 26th president of the United States.

1904 The World's Fair opens in St. Louis, Missouri.

1914 Mother's Day becomes an official holiday celebrated on the second Sunday in May.

1900   1905   1910   1915   1920

1903 Wilbur and Orville Wright make the first successful powered flight in an airplane.

1908 Ford introduces the Model T car.

1917 The United States joins the fighting in World War I.

ABOUT THE AUTHOR

Jane A. Schott has heard many memories of the early 1900s from her father, grandparents, and other relatives and friends. "I visited the old houses and barns. I saw the toys, furniture, and machines in museums and antique shops. I studied old photographs and read history books. Putting all these things together," she explains, "helps me visualize what life was like for children then." A former elementary school teacher, Ms. Schott received her master's degree in education and works as a textbook editor. She hopes her book will help bring this era of history alive for young people. She has written one other book for Carolrhoda, *Will Rogers*.

PHOTO ACKNOWLEDGMENTS

The photographs in this book are reproduced through the courtesy of: New York State Historical Association, Cooperstown, front cover, p. 38; Minnesota Historical Society, back cover, p. 13; Archive Photos/Levick, pp. 1, 14, 15; Joseph J. Pennell Collection, Kansas Collection, University of Kansas Libraries, p. 2; courtesy of Rockefeller Archive Center, p. 5; reprinted with the permission of American Automobile Manufacturers Association, p. 6; The Western Reserve Historical Society, Cleveland, Ohio, p. 7; Missouri Historical Society, St. Louis, pp. 8, 9, 10 (photo by Dr. Charles Swap); Corbis-Bettmann, pp. 11, 18, 24; Cincinnati Museum Center, p. 12; Jane A. Schott, pp. 16, 26, 37, 48; Archive Photos, pp. 17, 22; Brown Brothers, Sterling, PA, 18463, pp. 19, 20, 23, 31, 33, 39; From the Collection of David R. Phillips, p. 21; American Stock Photography, p. 25; "Children of High Class," detail, photograph by Arnold Genthe, California Historical Society, FN-02357, p. 27; Library of Congress, p. 28; National Archives, neg. #102-LH-1056, p. 29; Theodore Roosevelt Collection, Harvard College Library, p. 30; Museum of History & Industry, p. 32; Florida State Archives, p. 34; State Historical Society of Wisconsin, negative #CF361, p. 35; State Historical Society of Missouri, Columbia, p. 36; Lejla Omerovic, pp. 40, 41.

THE STORY BEHIND
KWANZAA

MELISSA RAÉ SHOFNER

PowerKiDS
press™

New York

Published in 2020 by The Rosen Publishing Group, Inc.
29 East 21st Street, New York, NY 10010

First Edition

Editor: Tanya Dellaccio
Book Design: Reann Nye

Photo Credits: Cover, p. 1 Purestock/Getty Images; pp. 4, 6, 8, 12, 14, 16, 18, 20, 22 (background) Preto Perola/Shutterstock.com; pp. 5, 21 Hill Street Studios/DigitalVision/Getty Images; pp. 7, 19 Robert Abbott Sengstacke/Archive Photos/Getty Images; p. 9 Inti St. Clair/Photodisc/Getty Images; p. 11 Timothy R. Nichols/Shutterstock.com; p. 13 Sue Barr/Image Source/Getty Images; p. 15 Miami Herald/Tribune News Service/Getty Images; p. 17 SAUL LOEB/ AFP/Getty Images; p. 22 Guy Cali/Corbis/Getty Images.

Cataloging-in-Publication Data

Names: Shofner, Melissa Raé.
Title: The story behind Kwanzaa / Melissa Raé Shofner.
Description: New York : PowerKids Press, 2020. | Series: Holiday histories | Includes glossary and index.
Identifiers: ISBN 9781725300569 (pbk.) | ISBN 9781725300583 (library bound) | ISBN 9781725300576 (6pack)
Subjects: LCSH: Kwanzaa–Juvenile literature.
Classification: LCC GT4403.R43 2020 | DDC 394.2612–dc23
Manufactured in the United States of America

CPSIA Compliance Information: Batch #CSPK19. For Further Information contact Rosen Publishing, New York, New York at 1-800-237-9932.

CONTENTS

Seven Special Days

Kwanzaa is a **celebration** of African American **culture** and history. People gather together to sing, dance, and eat. The holiday is seven days long. Each of the seven days stands for a different principle, or important value, in African culture. It's celebrated from December 26 to January 1.

Honoring Culture

Kwanzaa was first celebrated in 1966. A teacher named Dr. Maulana Karenga decided to create the holiday. He studied and taught African American history in California. African Americans have been **discriminated** against for a long time. Because of this, he wanted to celebrate their **accomplishments**.

A Mix of Traditions

The name "Kwanzaa" comes from words that mean "first fruits" in Swahili, a language spoken by some African peoples. The **traditions** of the holiday come from **harvest** celebrations from different African cultures. Dr. Karenga mixed them together to create Kwanzaa.

Seven Values

A candleholder called a kinara holds seven candles—one for each night of Kwanzaa. On the first day, a person celebrating lights a black candle. This **symbolizes** the first principle—*umoja,* or unity. Families talk about how to be **united** as a family and a community.

Team Effort

The second day's principle is *kujichagulia,* or **self-determination**. Families talk about how to speak up and work for themselves. The third day of Kwanzaa celebrates collective responsibility, or how to work as a team and help others solve their problems. This is also called *ujima.*

Continuing Success

The fourth principle is *ujamaa*, which means cooperative economics. This means African American communities creating and supporting businesses together. The fifth day honors purpose, or *nia*. Families talk about working together to build and support their communities.

Believing in Each Other

The sixth day of Kwanzaa celebrates *kuumba,* or creativity. People talk about how they can create a better world. The seventh and final day celebrates faith, or *imani.* This day is for believing in one's community and the people in it.

Seven Symbols

There also are seven symbols for Kwanzaa, including the kinara. *Mazao*, the fruits and vegetables eaten during the holiday, symbolize crops. The *mkeka* is a straw mat on which all of the other items are placed. It symbolizes tradition. Each child is symbolized by a *vibunzi*, or ear of corn.

19

The *mishumaa saba* are the seven candles that sit on the kinara—one black, three red, and three green. The *kikomba cha umoja* is a cup everyone drinks from. It symbolizes unity. *Zawadi* are gifts. Each person gets a gift, usually handmade, during Kwanzaa.

An Important Holiday

There are many different things that make Kwanzaa an important holiday. Families come together and talk about the seven principles and symbols. Each day, they learn and share more about their culture and community. During Kwanzaa, African Americans **reflect** on the past and make goals for the future.

GLOSSARY

accomplishment: Something done successfully.

celebration: A party or something special or enjoyable done for an important event or holiday.

culture: The beliefs and ways of life of a certain group of people.

discriminate: To treat someone differently than others.

harvest: Crops after they've been gathered. Also the act of gathering crops.

reflect: To think about.

self-determination: The freedom to make your own choices.

symbolize: To stand for something else.

tradition: A way of thinking, behaving, or doing something that's been used by people in a particular society for a long time.

united: Made up of people working together.

INDEX

WEBSITES

Due to the changing nature of Internet links, PowerKids Press has developed an online list of websites related to the subject of this book. This site is updated regularly. Please use this link to access the list: www.powerkidslinks.com/HH/kwanzaa